MY BURDEN
MY BLESSING

MY BURDEN
MY BLESSING

EDWARDS

XULON PRESS

Xulon Press
555 Winderley Pl, Suite 225
Maitland, FL 32751
407.339.4217
www.xulonpress.com

© 2024 by Edwards

All rights reserved solely by the author. The author guarantees all contents are original and do not infringe upon the legal rights of any other person or work. No part of this book may be reproduced in any form without the permission of the author.

Due to the changing nature of the Internet, if there are any web addresses, links, or URLs included in this manuscript, these may have been altered and may no longer be accessible. The views and opinions shared in this book belong solely to the author and do not necessarily reflect those of the publisher. The publisher therefore disclaims responsibility for the views or opinions expressed within the work.

Unless otherwise indicated, Scripture quotations taken from the New American Standard Bible (NASB). Copyright © 1960, 1962, 1963, 1968, 1971, 1972, 1973, 1975, 1977, 1995 by The Lockman Foundation. Used by permission. All rights reserved.

Paperback ISBN-13: 979-8-86850-142-5
Hard Cover ISBN-13: 979-8-86850-192-0
Ebook ISBN-13: 979-8-86850-143-2

EPIGRAPH

If I can touch the heart of one person with my book, then I believe that is the person God wanted to touch. My story is for the heart and soul of the saved and the unsaved.

I think we are all hungry for a reassuring sign that God still cares for his children on this planet. You will find that reassurance here.

- Mollie Edwards

DEDICATION

To my son and daughter who suffered through this ordeal at a tender age. Bill and Darcie Edwards, I dedicate this book to you.

To their Father Henry William Edwards (Hank) who in deep pain accepted Jesus as his Savior. 1938-2007.

To my precious Grandchildren, Sarah, William, Lauryn, Leah, Allie, and Dustin.

To Hank's sister, Sharon Edwards, fondly called Auntie Sharon.

To the communities of Salinas, Carmel, Pacific Grove, Monterey, Seaside, Marina, Big Sur,

Who prayed for Ehren and Prayer chains that went as far as Japan.

To all of those that helped Ehren you know who you are, you have never been forgotten.

Especially dedicated to our Son Ehren David who endured eight long years of suffering. Through all of that God allowed him to bring people closer to knowing Father, Son and Holy Spirit. Ehren David Edwards definitely had a mission from God. His presence on this Earth was in a form of a Prophecy by a well-known Catholic Priest.

"Ehren Will Usher in Second Coming of Jesus Our Lord."

BIOGRAPHY

Mollie Edwards

Mollie Edwards is a native Californian, born and raised on the San Francisco Peninsula.

She married her childhood sweetheart in 1960, had two children, and then went on to several careers.

First, she went back to college and earned a registered nurse's license for the State of California. She worked as a nurse for several years and then stayed home to have her third child.

Mollie later decided to turn her love of sports cars into a career. She teamed up with a friend and bought and sold classic 356 Porsches for several years.

Next, she turned her interest in buying and selling property into a career. Mollie was so successful in negotiating several lucrative sales that she and her husband were able to construct apartment buildings. Ultimately, she earned her California Real Estate License. Married to a contractor, everything went very smoothly.

In 1986, Mollie went to the heart of Africa as a nurse and lay minister. She helped set up an immunization clinic for babies through the age of five. The highlight of her African trip was to be asked to preach to about 400 natives in a tiny village in Uganda.

At age 50, she took up horseback riding and then barrel racing, which took her to the finals in Reno, Nevada. She remained an active horsewoman in Northern California for many years.

Mollie is a self-described "people person" and enjoyed volunteering at a local rest home for many years. She has been involved in several grass-roots groups that have worked with the homeless.

In 2020, after living in many other towns across the U.S., Mollie moved to Johnstown, Pennsylvania. Her vintage fourplex is about three hours from her son Bill's home. She chose a comfortable, accessible place she loves where the people are friendly, the land is beautiful and in the mountains. She loves the snow in winter and warmer days in summer. She is very happy in her adopted State.

She has been a widow since 2007. Mollie is the mother of three children, six grandchildren and four great grandchildren.

INTRODUCTION

This is a true story from my heart to yours. It is my story and very personal.

Three days after my son's drowning accident, I was standing in my walk-in closet when I heard a voice. It wasn't a thought or "voice in my head," but a booming voice. The source was external.

"A book will be written, My Burden, My Blessing," I heard.

All I could do was ask aloud, "What do you mean, a book will be written? Our son is dying. What do you mean?"

There was no response.

More than four decades later, through the process of writing this book, I'm happy to tell you I found the answer to my question. I found the meaning of God's message to me that day in the closet. I know that God asked me to write my story for you. My burden was I wanted to tell the world immediately of the Voice of God and the Vision.

- Mollie Edwards

TABLE OF CONTENTS

Chapter 1: A Story 4 Decades in the Making 1

Chapter 2: Ehren, our fair-haired, blue-eyed boy 7

Chapter 3: The Accident 11

Chapter 4: Father Paul 19

Chapter 5: Finding Hope 23

Chapter 6: Hope Takes Over 27

Chapter 7: The Surprising Need for Balance 31

Chapter 8: How Our Marriage Survived 37

Chapter 9: How My Burden Became My Blessing 43

Chapter 10: 8 Ways to Find Comfort After Tragedy 51

Chapter 11: Where to Find Your Blessing 57

Chapter 1
A STORY 4 DECADES IN THE MAKING

There's something to be said for writing in God's time. He dictates when and what and how stories will be told. I learned this while stressing over the fact that this book must be written.

In 1996, I joined a boot-camp style writing class in hopes of creating this book. The teacher was a very accomplished writer.

Each of the 13 people in my class were supposed to tell the others about their book. As my turn came around, I didn't want to blurt it all out ¾ the closet, the booming voice, questioning the voice.

As I was telling the whole class the part of the story where the voice boomed down saying, "A book will be written," bells began to chime.

Over and over, the bells chimed as if someone was in a church belfry going crazy ringing the bells. It was a shock to me, and I believed it might be a sign that this truly was time to tell my story.

I wrote eight chapters. The teacher and my fellow students critiqued each chapter. Still, I had no book.

At that time, I wrote, "This story could not have been told 20 years ago or even 12 years ago when Ehren actually died. You see, I have been 'composting' for all those years. At least that is what I have been told.

"Getting everything in perspective, plus the fact of just letting something of this magnitude of happenings rest for a while and come at it at a less emotional time in my life."

Despite taking a writing class to learn how to write my own story satisfactorily, and despite the fact that I can't recall failing at much in my life, I could not create a book.

Perhaps, for a mother, no matter how much time passes, the tragic loss of her youngest child can be too emotional to convey.

However, I believe the lessons learned are universal and the emotional value of this story will resonate with many people. It is important for my own family to have this legacy. I can tell you, as this book is completed 40 years after Ehren's 1984 death, these memories are as painful, joyous, and fresh as the day they happened.

A vision of doom before tragedy

I can still remember driving the scenic Highway 68 that stretches from Salinas, California, to Carmel, California. All the fields in the Salinas area were filled with lettuce plants the color of green gold.

Lettuce is not only beautiful to look at, but it brings some good dollars to the hard-working people in the agricultural industry.

I was in my car heading toward my favorite haunt, Carmel Beach, when I had this extraordinary vision of a slot machine with numbers whirring around. It was as if it had something to do with my number coming up. The vision gave me a sense of doom.

It took several days to shake that feeling of doom. Shortly, I would experience tragedy that seemed to be without end, and I believe this feeling of doom on Highway 68 was a precursor.

Until then, my life had been fairly normal and mainstream. Born in 1941, I lived on the San Francisco Peninsula all my life. I married my childhood sweetheart at age 18. We had two lovely children: one girl and one boy.

I decided at that point to do something for myself. I went back to finish college. I took the registered nursing course, became an RN, and got a great job on the Monterey Peninsula. But shortly after, I became very ill.

I stayed home for a while and then decided to have another child. There would be ten years between this child and my last child.

Ehren is born

This little trailer called Ehren was the apple of all of our eyes. He was the smartest of all three of my kids. He did not talk early, but he knew exactly what you were saying and what you wanted. And he was gorgeous.

I quit being a rabble rouser

About three months before Ehren was born I had accepted Christ Jesus into my heart my life my all. Not that I was an atheist, but I had strayed from the church and really had been seeking some sort of spiritual enlightenment.

All my friends at the time were a little worried about me. I guess they thought I was going to get into some sort of weird cult. So, unknown to me, they were praying constantly for me.

During one prayer session that I had been invited to, I decided that I was not going to question God anymore. I wanted to cease being a rabble rouser. I just wanted to take the Bible on pure faith and have God help me with the rest.

Of course, I didn't know at that point that I would be tested to the highest degree this old life can dish out. Tragedy ultimately gave me a new understanding of life. Over time, I have learned that life is really about spiritual unfolding that is personal and spellbinding.

Chapter 2
EHREN, OUR FAIR-HAIRED, BLUE-EYED BOY

Ehren was gorgeous and very smart for just two years old. He was not extremely verbal, but he understood much of our conversations with him. If he wanted to go swimming, he would go into his bedroom, open the correct door, pull out his swim trunks, and hold them up with such a happy gleam in his eyes.

He also loved music. We had an antique player piano. I happened to find the Mickey Mouse March on a roll. Ehren would pull up an ottoman, sit down and manage to pump the pedals to play Mickey's March over and over again.

And he was a rascal, always giving us chills as he dared to take chances. I'll never forget his hijinks.

I remember one day driving from Salinas to Menlo Park along Blood Alley to visit my folks. Guess I was going a little fast because along came the highway patrol.

The policeman pulled me over.

"Out of the car, ma'am, and bring your license with you," he said.

I had to park along the right side of the highway, get out on the driver's side, and meet him on the other side of the car. Funny things that run through a person's mind when they are pulled over by the cops. All I could do was look down at my size 8 1/2 shoe and say to myself, "God, what big feet I have."

Ehren was in the front seat. He was just a little guy at the time, younger than 18 months. He managed to open the door while I was talking with the officer. By the time I saw him, Ehren was running into the traffic lane.

The rest of the memory is a blur, but one of us got to Ehren first and scooped him up and out of harm's way. I didn't get a ticket that day. The policeman and I were both rattled and parted with grateful hearts that Ehren was safe.

Another time, we were at our summer cabin at San Clemente Rancho. It was a balmy day in Carmel Valley. The air was heavy with the musky smell of warm earth. The sky was the color of infinite meadows of Heaven. Ehren and I were walking along, hand-in-hand. We were walking near the swimming pool, and in a split second he had walked right into the pool. Fortunately, I had a tight hold on his hand, and he wasn't hurt this time.

Ehren, our fair-haired, blue-eyed boy

He had so many near misses for such a little baby it was almost as though drama was just in his path.

Once, at the Rancho, Ehren was playing on our deck. We built it over a creek. The deck had fences all around. I could not have been more than 10 feet away when I glanced up and saw that he had found a way to get under the fence. He was dangling, ready to fall on top of a cement pile. Again, a near miss for our little boy!

Then there was the time Ehren drank some Clorox while a babysitter was taking care of him. He was rushed to the hospital.

At day care, they made him sit in the bad chair because he was hitting kids on the head with his toys.

To us, he was a sweet, loving child.

The morning of his last escapade, he had gotten some cheese balls from the refrigerator. The cheese balls were wrapped up like candy. By the time I got to the kitchen, Ehren had devoured about six and was throwing eggs on the floor.

Chapter 3
THE ACCIDENT

Serra Village sits between Salinas, which is known as the lettuce capital of the world, and Carmel and Monterey, which are well known for beaches and restaurants.

My husband and father built most of Serra Village, including office buildings, the fire department and highway patrol headquarters.

Everyone knew each other. Many other young families had moved in, and we were all just starting out in life. It was a beautiful area with trees and rolling hills that went right up to the vast open space that was Fort Ord at the time.

Further South was Laguna Seca, and on a still day you could hear the drones of the race cars on the track.

The weather was just about perfect in the village each day. We were far enough South to avoid the Salinas fog. We also missed the fog that settled over Monterey Bay. We were living in the serene sun belt area.

Hank built us the best house in Serra Village, Salinas, California, in 1973. It had everything I had ever dreamed of in a home. Hank even built a great dark room for me. He also contracted for a swimming pool. I never thought I would have my own home with a pool.

I told Hank that I wanted a child-proof fence around the pool because we would never forgive ourselves if something happened. As a nurse, I was acutely aware of accidental drownings . . . of accidents, period.

The morning was sunny, as usual. Gert Kocek was in her kitchen washing pots and pans. Her kitchen was typical of all the 1976 kitchens in Serra Village. Dark wood cabinets, harvest gold appliances, and the shag rug in the dining area.

Gert was scrubbing away in her kitchen; all the windows and doors were tightly shut. Suddenly, a voice was ringing in her head: "Gert, go outside of your house." "GERT, GO OUTSIDE OF YOUR HOUSE."

The "voice" just kept getting louder.

At first, Gert thought she must be going crazy or having some sort of attack. Finally, she went to her backyard.

On that same beautiful, sunny morning, Hank, the kids and I were enjoying our first morning home from a vacation. We had gotten home the prior night.

The drapes were still down in the living room where I was talking on the phone to my next-door neighbor,

Susan. The sun was streaming through the large floor-to-ceiling windows in the kitchen.

Ehren had been in the refrigerator eating cheese balls and throwing eggs on the floor. I put him in his beloved play yard, which was alongside the house.

There, he had Tonka trucks, fire engines, toys galore. Ehren loved his yard and toys, and I could hear his little two-year-old voice attempt to make car noises. I enjoyed his little jibber jabber as I was talking on the phone.

This particular morning, well into my conversation with Susan, I noticed silence outside.

I quickly laid the phone down, saying into the air I would be right back. (Phones were attached to cords in those days. We stayed in one place to talk, limited by the length of the phone cord.)

Gert heard my screams over the fence. Susan heard my screams over the phone. Wounded animal sounds emitted from my throat.

Ehren was floating in our pool.

My screams were now pleas to Heaven: "Please, God! Don't take my baby!"

I was in the water pulling him out when a deep, resonant voice boomed down to me from above. This voice was not something talking to me in my head. It was a voice that to this day I can recall exactly. I remember the direction it came from and the timbre of the voice. It wasn't a spooky sound, nor did it sound human. It resonated deeply, as if someone was speaking from the bottom of a barrel.

The voice simply said, "Ehren will come back to you. Ehren will be restored."

In spit seconds, I was acutely aware of the total dichotomy life had just given me. On one hand, my precious son's lifeless body was a parent's worst nightmare. This angst was the worst thing that could happen. On the other hand, I experienced something that I instinctively knew was so beyond this world that it was beyond my understanding. I heard the voice and felt that Ehren was being taken care of totally . . . with total, intense love.

I struggled to pull Ehren out of the pool. At the same moment, Gert was screaming over my back fence, "I can resuscitate! I can resuscitate!"

Gert arrived quickly and began working on Ehren. I called 911. I remember that we never bothered to put the house numbers on our front porch. I ran out of the house to the front yard. I needed to make sure the fire department found us.

A glistening throne appeared

I found myself sitting in the street, within the curve of our driveway . . . waiting.

The weather was beautiful, blue skies, balmy air, bright sunshine flooded over me. All of a sudden, with my eyes wide open, I saw something that certainly was not of this world: a huge, glowing white object that looked like some sort of throne.

I really do not have words to adequately describe it. I perceived the throne to have many jewels encrusted deep within, glowing and shimmering. This "not of the world happening" appeared to me for only several seconds, but from that moment forward I felt a peace that truly passes all understanding. I felt such love for friends and family.

That was not all. On this throne, I felt a very definite presence. I quickly knew it to be a much higher power that could only be our Creator. Suspended on this throne, I saw a white bundle. I perceived this bundle to be Ehren. I felt that this glowing white bundle was being nurtured. I did not see arms encompassing the bundle, but I very definitely felt that nurturing was taking place.

This suspended bundle was lifted and advanced forward in an offertory gesture.

From that moment, my life changed forever.

I felt an intense love and caring toward my friends and family. My nature was immediately softer.

Through it all, I was coherent. My body felt as if it weighed a ton. I thought my heart would literally break into pieces.

The ambulance arrived

When the ambulance arrived, I could not bring myself to get up off the street and go to the backyard.

I remember someone brought me a blanket. I thought that was odd because they did not put it over me; they just held it up.

Later, I found out they were shielding me from a creep who had made his way to my backyard with a big TV camera. Evidently, when I called 911, the call went out over the airways. A television reporter picked up my call on his scanner and came to our house. My friends guessed I might just deck him if I saw him. Yes, I think I really could have decked him.

With friends surrounding me and God's presence so very real at this time, I experienced a strange dichotomy. This feeling of joy and love in the midst of tragedy was overwhelming, to say the least.

When I tried to explain this dichotomy to people soon after the drowning, you can imagine some of their reactions. I very soon learned to keep many things to myself.

People don't like talking about or exploring some spiritual matters that cannot be explained.

I am sure, however, that God had a definite plan for my life and for little Ehren's life.

Ehren is revived at the hospital

Ehren arrived at the hospital dead on arrival (DOA). The doctors probably worked on him longer than if it had been an adult in the same condition, trying to restore his young life.

By the time I arrived at the hospital, they had him hooked up to the breathing machine because they had revived him.

They would not let me see him, and that is one of my worst memories. Today, I don't believe that would happen. I think hearing the voice of a mother or father can impact the healing process.

Ehren was in a coma. Finally, they let me see him. His pupils were enormously dilated.

I spoke to my son, but could not pick him up and hold him. There were tubes in every part of his little body.

Ehren actually said a few words. In his 23-month-old voice, he said, "Mommy! Eyes, Mommy!"

His vision had to be gone at this point. My son couldn't see.

The nurses escorted me out, and to this day I don't remember if they let me see him again that night.

I believed some of his brain must be intact because he was able to discern that his eyes were not working.

Chapter 4
FATHER PAUL

Several months before Ehren's accident, a pastor had come through our little community of Serra Village.

One particular clear, sunny day, Pastor Paul Danielson came calling. He said he represented the local Episcopalian Church. He asked some of the usual questions. Did we have a church?

I told him that my husband had been raised Episcopalian and that I had gone to the Presbyterian Church in Menlo Park.

Father Paul was a tall, lanky, soft-spoken man. He drove an old VW bus and dressed like a poor Oxford scholar. He was extremely intelligent, and you knew the moment you saw him that he loved being a pastor. You could tell without a doubt that he loved the Lord very much.

I remember having a wonderful conversation with him that day and promising that I would drop by to hear a Sunday sermon sometime.

MY BURDEN MY BLESSING

I did not keep that promise right away. In fact, I did not see him again until he came to the hospital the night of Ehren's accident.

I remember Father Paul coming into that horrible waiting room and embracing Hank and me. We gathered in a huddle with bent heads and started praying.

Father Paul had such a way with words. He brought you right into his prayers. I could literally feel God's presence in that hideous cubicle of a waiting room.

Father Paul became a welcome part of our spiritual life and part of our family for the next eight years.

Hank and I started going to church. Many times, I would go alone. Hank was not up for a big commitment to the church. He kept so many feelings inside of himself instead of sharing with friends, as I did.

I know now that I could not have made it through that first night without all the prayers and support I received from Father Paul.

I did not tell him about the voice that boomed down from the heavens, nor did I tell him about what I saw in the sky. I kept all that inside for three days, and then I felt I had to share it with Father Paul. Why? Because I believed something extraordinary had happened. I desperately did not want people to think I was crazy or off balance.

On that third day, after many more prayers with Father Paul and much heartache concerning Ehren's state, I finally told Father Paul about what I had seen and heard before the ambulance arrived.

I will never forget the look on that man's face. His soft eyes and calm demeanor took on such a mollescent quality. This man was already soft spoken, but he went beyond that as he absorbed what I said.

He looked at me for what I thought was an eternity. He looked into my eyes with soul looking into soul and said, "Mollie, you were blessed with a vision."

Those words sent electricity through my body. It was the confirmation I needed. I knew that something extraordinary had happened.

Sharing My Vision

Over the years, I learned not to share my experiences—my visions—with just anyone. Sometimes, I had to learn the hard way that people were not receptive to religious experiences. I since have shared only sparingly the "booming voice" and the white glowing throne image that appeared as my son lay dying.

I only share my story when people are genuinely curious and ask about the tragedy and how I was able to cope. Most who have heard the story have said they are sincerely blessed, and they have always left the conversation a little happier.

Several of my friends said I should be on Phil Donahue Show to share my story. I never felt led to do anything like this. Four decades later I now could do that, but Phil is not around anymore.

Chapter 5
FINDING HOPE

I was on my own during those first nights and days at the hospital. Hank stayed at home except for the very first night.

In that bleak waiting room, I met the most memorable Hispanic family. Their uncle had suffered a debilitating heart attack. There must have been 15 extended family members keeping a vigil for him.

We all became friends and prayed daily for each other. It turned out that the young nephew worked in the produce section of the grocery store I frequented.

He, his wife, and I became prayer warriors for our family members.

Over the ensuring years, I would occasionally see him in the produce department, and we would catch up on family news. The young man's name was Genaro, and he was such a loving, caring human being. I was proud to call him my friend.

MY BURDEN MY BLESSING

One evening about a week after Ehren's accident, Genaro and his family and extended family shared the most wonderful prayer with me.

HOPE

Hope is reaching out for God
And knowing He is there;
Hope is searching for release,
And finding it though prayer.
Hope is happiness and joy,
And rainbows in the sky.
Hope is feeling God is near
When you begin to cry.
Hope is looking for a dream
That someday will come true.
Hope is waiting on the Lord,
When your days are sad and blue.
Hope is wishing for a star
That will bring you peace and light.
Hope is striving for God's love
To uphold you day and night! (Author Unknown)

That night I drove home from the hospital to be with the rest of my family for a few hours. I was remembering bits and pieces of the poem. "Reaching out for God," "Hope is feeling God is near," and of course, "Waiting on the Lord" played back in my mind as I drove.

I am so glad the freeway was almost empty and the night very dark because what was to come would have probably disconcerted some driver who chanced to look in my car window.

I took only one year of Spanish, but what came out of my mouth those few miles from Salinas as I drove home through the canyon astounds me to this day.

What is a prayer language?

Spanish words tumbled out of my mouth. It was as if I was pouring my heart out to the Lord and he was really hearing me.

There was a certain rhythm and cadence to the prose. I thought it sounded beautiful, but I did not understand a single word. Later, I recalled a few words: Dios, Arco, and a few more that I have now forgotten.

The next few days, I shared the words and this experience with friends and pastors. I found out "Dios" was Spanish for God, and "arco" means rainbow. Both would be significant in Ehren's life in years to come.

When I shared this unusual occurrence with a pastor friend, he told me that I had been given a prayer language. I had never heard of such a thing. "What in the world is a prayer language?" I asked.

The pastor said it is something that is very Biblical and is a praise language for God.

Over the next eight years, I probably used the prayer language three or four times in various prayer meetings. I never felt the language was to be something on display or over-used. I felt it was up to God when and where I would use this language gift.

Chapter 6
HOPE TAKES OVER

Even though Ehren was revived, he was not the little boy we all knew. We loved him desperately, but we were all changed human beings as a result of the tragedy. My oldest child, Darcie, was a young teenager when the accident happened, and she was devastated. Darcie had been "a little mother" to Ehren, and her world spiraled into pain and sadness as she faced our family's new, tormented reality. It took a great deal of time to begin to heal, individually and as a family.

We all had a difficult time coping with Ehren's suffering and our own. To this day, we rarely talk about the accident and those eight years.

Ehren's tiny body assumed many different positions after the drowning and resuscitation. He was flaccid at the beginning. Then, his arms and legs became more and more spastic for a prolonged period. This resulted in a position called opthopthesis, which pulled him backwards with his feet almost touching his head.

Ehren never uttered a word again. He could not see, sit up or walk. He was in what is commonly called a vegetative state.

Taking a Stand for a Child Who Couldn't

I practically lived at the hospital for days and weeks on end. This continued for months.

After the accident, Ehren had to be monitored on intravenous fluids; he was given no solid food. The doctors wanted me to put Ehren in an institution, but I would not. They made me visit two institutions, and I sobbed so hard at each place that there was no chance any facility was going to be an option for my son.

We took Ehren home and cared for him. The wisdom of God's plan for me to become a nurse was revealed. Clearly, His plan is always perfect.

We took Ehren to doctor after doctor, seeking any chance of a cure or improvement. If there was an answer for Ehren, we wanted to find it. Early on, I took him to Stanford University Hospital where a red-headed, freckle-faced young doctor said Ehren would never swallow again because his gag reflex would never return.

"Until you are God, don't tell me that," I said, defiantly.

Ehren's gag reflex did return.

If I had ceased to believe . . . if I had ever doubted God's desire to restore my son, I can't imagine how I would have gotten through those eight traumatic years.

Sustained by our belief in God, we kept Ehren at home and lovingly cared for him. Gradually, I started feeding him through the mouth with a tube-like apparatus that had a plunger on one end. He did swallow! I pureed his food and fed him bite by bite, day after day, year after year.

Ehren cried a lot in those early days. His very high-pitched cry was very indicative of a brain-injured child.

I remember longing to hear his normal cry. And I yearned to hear his footsteps paddling down the hallways in his little sleeper pajamas, running toward us to say, "good morning!"

Life on the Roller Coaster

The doctors were very perplexed as Ehren seemed to be on some sort of roller coaster ride. He would seem to be getting better, then the next minute, he would lose ground.

One morning in particular, the doctor called me at home.

"Ehren is losing the battle fast. He has internal bleeding from taking in the chlorine from the pool. I don't think he will make it this time, Mollie."

I totally lost it. Sobbing . . . animal sounds . . . plain and simple grieving . . . these pitiful sounds emitted from my innermost being.

I had forgotten that the washing machine repairman was scheduled to repair my machine that morning. The doorbell rang and there he was, and there I was, totally losing it.

All I could do was show him where the machine was and go back to my grieving.

Chapter 7
THE SURPRISING NEED FOR BALANCE

Shortly after the accident, I knelt beside my bed to pray. For some reason, I didn't ask, "Why me, God?" Instead, I asked for balance in my life.

Now, looking back, I realize how important that particular prayer really was. I was directed or guided in some way to ask God for balance.

When I look back, I believe one of the reasons I became so very close to the church during those days was to balance the terrible tragedy that had occurred and the mission we all had to maintain every day. That sad mission was our struggle to deal with a child in a vegetative state. I became a lay minister in our Church. I served communion. I was sent to local Bishop with recommendation to become one of first women Episcopalian Priests. I did not follow through.

For eight years, as Ehren lingered, our family endured a roller coaster of emotions. How could we ever be really happy while Ehren was suffering?

God sent help when I needed it most

Amazingly, God sent help in remarkable ways.

For instance, one day my doorbell rang. There stood six of my good friends and neighbors. They had been at a Great Books meeting in my neighborhood and had felt a strange sensation that I needed them at that moment.

Most of those women were Christians. They took one look at me and said, "Tell us what is happening, Mollie."

All I could manage to get out was, "Doctor says he's dying."

We all headed for the family room and made a circle of chairs around the coffee table. Someone started us off with a prayer. The prayers kept going around the group; they just kept flowing out.

Certainly, no one pressured me to pray, but when the circle of prayers ended at me, I felt the sudden urge to speak out and pray.

What came out of my mouth was a long, flowing prayer that sounded like poetry. This happened without any thought on my part. It just came out that way.

The prayer was coming from deep, deep pain from the depth of my soul.

Everyone was flabbergasted, including me.

I couldn't believe I had actually spoken all those words in perfect prose. I remember the feeling more than the words I said that day. Too bad no one recorded that prayer. I do remember that I praised God and thanked him for the vision.

Even more awesome than my prayer was the phone call that came immediately after. The phone just happened to be on top of the round oak coffee table where we were seated. The table had been my grandmother's dining table years earlier.

The doctor was calling. "Mollie," he said, "I don't know what is happening here, but Ehren rallied just seconds ago, and he is doing much better."

God Reveals the Vision of the White Throne

Another time, my good friend Barbara came to my door. I had been having a very difficult day. My spirits were low, and I was asking God a lot of questions through prayer.

Barbara rang our doorbell, and when I answered she immediately asked me if I would like to read something uplifting.

"Yes," I said without hesitation. Then I told her about my questions and the bad day I was having.

Barbara presented me with a sweet little white book that had been hers as a child. She told me to keep it as long as I felt I needed it, and then she wanted it back, since it was a family keepsake.

The whole book was about God on a glowing white throne!

Barbara remembered the vision I had the day of Ehren's accident, and she found that story. We stood there in the entry hall reading this little story, and at the end we just looked at each other and hugged.

Shirley Prayed Me Through

Shirley, my lifelong friend, helped me through the eight painful years after Ehren's accident in a very special way. Here's how.

After Ehren's accident, Shirley had a dream so profound that she went to her pastor to discuss it with him. The dream gave her a distinct word: pattern.

The pastor confirmed that the dream involved the community, and he said Shirley would be a very large part of something to do with Ehren.

That dream came to pass, and Shirley never abandoned Ehren or me for eight long years. She called me every morning and said, "OK, let's get to praying." She would literally pray me through the day. Those prayers gave me the strength I needed to survive.

Our prayers always started out with a forgiveness of sins prayer. Things seen and unseen. Then we would put on the armor of Jesus, give lots of thanks in all instances, and then I would make it until the following day.

There are not enough words or thanks for all Shirley did for me in the late 1970s all the way to 1984. She believed in what she was doing, and we all believed a miracle was going to occur.

Shirley is a homemaker, grandmother, and wife of a retired dentist. Since those days, she has battled lymphoma and won. She comes from the Midwest town of Fargo, North Dakota. She is a beautiful person, inside and out.

Sadly my friend Shirley did die several years ago. She will never be forgotten.

Helping others, helping yourself

They say when you are having great difficulty, the best thing to do is get out of yourself and help another. I did just that for at least five years at Casa Serena. I never regretted a minute of my time there. There was always a blessing around the corner.

I remember my first day at Casa Serena. Shirley, who got me into this volunteer work, called me.

"I can't make it today, Mollie. You will be just fine," Shirley said.

Well, I got to Casa Serena, one of Salinas' so-called "finest facilities," and the nurses had most of the patients in the Rec room. Most were in wheelchairs; some were in ordinary straight back chairs. I thought I would start with a prayer.

"Wouldn't hurt," I thought. "Here I go. Straight into telling them about how much Jesus loved them and what a great day this was."

But I was trying to talk louder than one of the patients, Frankie.

Frankie was babbling nonsense and talking about rats on the floor.

"Frankie," I said, "Pleeez be quiet. We are speaking to Jesus now. Let's be real quiet."

I rambled on for what might have been one of the longest prayers of my life. I ended as I always had in prayer groups with, "And we pray all of this in the precious name of our Lord Jesus."

Frankie, in the most clear, concise voice, said, "That is the best prayer I have ever heard."

We all need approval occasionally, and I found it in the most unlikely places!

Chapter 8
HOW OUR MARRIAGE SURVIVED

In addition to volunteer work that got me out of the house occasionally, my support system included many friends, pastors, and priests—all who were willing counselors. Hank didn't have friends to talk with, and he didn't have a strong relationship with God. Hank had a very hard time dealing with Ehren's pain. He did work very hard to make our business a success.

When a tragedy occurs, the dynamics that go on between a husband and wife are off the charts. Statistics say when a couple has a tragedy of the magnitude we did, the odds are totally against saving the marriage. In five years, most couples divorce.

I know why.

The core reason: each person is hurting so greatly that it is all but impossible to comfort each other.

What got us through? Why did my marriage survive? We were open and hopeful. We kept believing there was another side to life that we had yet to discover. We also believed there was truly some other process operating behind the scenes—a higher power.

We came through a tragedy that many others would have faced by just pulling up the sheets and saying, "That's it!"

When things got tough, we didn't give up on our son or our marriage.

Our Dream House

Hank and I scrimped, saved, and borrowed to get enough money to buy three lovely acres in the Salinas foothills a year before Ehren's accident. At this point, we had three children: Darcie, Bill, and one-year-old Ehren. (Ten years separated Bill and Ehren; Darcie was our oldest child.)

The best architect in the area drew up plans for the house. He also helped us find many pieces of furniture.

Then the world was ripped from under our feet. Our precious child drowned, was pronounced dead and was revived, only to live trapped inside a body that would never function normally again.

We decided to continue building the new house, but we did so with little vigor or excitement. It turned out to be a blessing to have pushed forward since the home was much larger than our other home. Gratefully, the new house could accommodate all the handicap

How Our Marriage Survived

items we needed for Ehren and the continuous flow of people that were destined to come into our lives.

This wonderful home in the hills of Salinas had seven different levels. Hank built it so it nestled right into the hill without making a cut in the hill. He saved all of the giant oak trees and planted all indigenous species of plant life.

We had decks and walkways all around the house. In one of the decks, we built a river stone fire pit. The whole house was cedar outside and inside.

To the casual observer, we had it all.

I opened our doors to Young Life groups. We had Christmas parties every year. One-hundred twenty-five teenagers just melted into the woodwork in our large home. I really tried to make things as normal as possible for Darcie and Bill, who were both teenagers by then. They had their own bedrooms and a lot of space to get away from some of the tough day-to-day things that went on with Ehren.

We hired respite caregivers to come in and help me with Ehren's care. They were blessings to our family because they were marvelous human beings.

Our construction business flourished. Jobs came in at a rapid pace. We felt God was really watching over us.

Insurance did not cover the money we paid to hire caregivers. Our savings and our home were gone by the time of Ehren's death. People came to our door offering help. I always refused as I was too embarrassed to admit we needed help.

Toward the end of the eight years, just months before Ehren passed, the money that had been coming in on a regular basis dwindled to nothing.

Hank's father had offered us a small amount of money. I thought that was fine since my parents had given us money to start our new home. Why couldn't Hank's father help us keep it?

My parents were not rich. They saved all their lives and were extremely happy to help me. I was their only child. They delighted in seeing Hank and me progress. They also saw how important it was to me to keep Ehren at home and have space around us.

Hank's father, on the other hand, had millions.

When I found out Hank had turned down his father's offer, I wasn't completely surprised. Hank had been psychologically beaten up by his father all his life. If Hank had accepted, the money would have come with strings attached, and Hank chose not to deal with his father's demeaning nature.

I thought I would be the bigger person and try to explain that we really did need the money to keep Ehren at home. I phoned Hank's father and got the tongue lashing of my life. Bottom line: I was told I was never welcome in his home again because I had asked for money.

My father-in-law's second wife was telling people Ehren was never going to make it, "so why help a dying cause?"

Looking back, I realize I should have known better than to ask Hank's father for anything. My father-in-law had never expressed kindness or appreciation. Moreover, he treated Hank, his mother, and sister badly. I should have known better. The pain of our situation was compounded by this unfortunate little family drama.

Hank Finds Jesus

Father Paul may not have gotten Hank to attend church every Sunday, but he had a lasting impact on my husband's life.

One day, Hank came home very sick. Ehren was back in the hospital, and I had a prayer group going on at our house. Hank walked in the house, passed by all of us gals and plopped down on a chair on the deck. We could see him through the picture window. He was talking incoherently.

I went to Hank, felt his forehead and realized he was extremely feverish.

Returning to the group, I explained that my husband was sick. I asked for prayers on Hank's behalf, and I mentioned that Hank never had asked the Lord to come into his life. "I don't really know where he stands in his belief," I said.

We all prayed hard for Hank. It was obvious to us all that he was suffering, but not just from the fever. I am sure grief was very high on the list as he called out for Ehren and Jesus repeatedly.

Shortly after the prayer, everyone said their goodbyes. I steered Hank to bed and asked him if there was anything I could do. He came out of his delirium long enough to say he wanted to ask Christ into his life. I told him I would be right back, and I got on the phone immediately to Father Paul.

Father Paul arrived minutes later.

It is a comfort to me that Hank accepted Jesus as his personal Savior that day, and I am grateful to the ladies in my prayer group and especially to Father Paul for his counsel and ever-timely assistance.

Chapter 9
HOW MY BURDEN BECAME MY BLESSING

My daily prayers with Shirley, my prayer group with Father Paul, and my Bible study group led by Father Jim Nesbit all helped me survive the daily problems. Father Nesbit had an extraordinary prophecy for Ehren in the 1979s: "Ehren will usher in the second coming of Jesus Christ."

Days and months and years ticked by very slowly after Ehren's accident. Every day I was on watch for some sign of a divine miracle. Every day I thought about the voice that boomed down from Heaven as I was pulling Ehren out of the pool, the vision of the white throne, and the voice in the closet telling me a book would be written.

I never, ever gave up hope. I would invariably say to myself, "God told me Ehren would be restored."

Despite all the horrible things that happened, I constantly felt intensely blessed. No matter what happened on the toughest of days, something came along to uplift me. I managed to remain positive when people came to visit, and I sincerely had a positive feeling about Ehren's future.

I remember three times when Ehren responded to us during the eight years after his accident:

- Mr. Rogers' Neighborhood was on TV. Ehren managed to move and fall off his vibrating pad when he heard Mr. Rogers talk about the perils of swimming pools.

- One birthday, I was singing a little song that I had made up telling Ehren how much I loved him, and tears began streaming down his face.

- Once, during his pattern program, he said, "Momma." Everyone heard him say it.

I can't wait to tell you about his pattern program.

Our Self-Created Program, New Beginnings, Has Surprising Results

What could we do to help Ehren? I researched and discovered a unique therapy, worked with the church leaders I had befriended, and found a place to conduct the therapy sessions.

A physical therapist, a neurosurgeon and physiatrist, and a psychologist developed Doman-Delacato patterning therapy (DDPT) in the 1940s. Its core assumption: brain damage causes a blockage in the normal pattern of brain development. They believed the consequences of this blockage could be eliminated through "patterning" therapy exercises that attempted to rewire the brain.

Sometimes called "psychomotor patterning," this non-invasive therapy involved four adults who assist the child in an effort to induce the proper pattern of movement onto the central nervous system. For example, one person extends the child's left arm and right leg. Next, the opposite limbs are flexed. And so on.

We called Ehren's therapy, or patterning program, "New Beginnings," and the rainbow was our logo. Both were taken from Bible verses that had been revealed to me, especially through the prayer language God had given me.

Each day, I took Ehren to the local Catholic Book store. They provided a back room for his therapy. People volunteered through sign-up sheets, and they arrived at appointed times to help with Ehren's patterning therapy. In all, we spent about an hour a day.

Miraculously, Ehren attracted people from every religious denomination represented in Salinas—Catholic, Lutheran, Mormon, Episcopalian, Presbyterian and every faith community. Wonderful people signed up to help, and his patterning program schedule was always full. Journalists did stories. Volunteers met and fell in love with Ehren. They took up his cause, prayed for him, and loved him. Many people were changed forever.

New Beginnings was appropriately named. Some volunteers who worked with Ehren through his patterning program came to know Jesus Christ and asked Him into their hearts. Married couples who were ready to divorce were healed while working with Ehren. Pastors and priests dropped by to check on Ehren.

In turn, Ehren was stimulated verbally as well. People talked with him, encouraged him. Ehren wasn't put aside in a room, institutionalized or left alone just because he wasn't whole. Instead, we focused on him and engaged him, always believing his miracle—his restoration—was coming.

Through the New Beginnings program, something very special was always happening around him. Hope surrounded Ehren.

Ehren turned out to be a little minister. People came to help him, and they were helped. I am eternally grateful that people were led to Jesus Christ through Ehren's New Beginnings program. Many others had their faith in God the Father, Son, and Holy Spirit affirmed after interacting with Ehren.

I believe God's promise to me that day in the swimming pool was totally fulfilled. I was clearly told, "Ehren will come back to you. Ehren will be restored." The first part of the promise was fulfilled when Ehren was resuscitated. Rather than perishing that day, he was with us for eight more years, during which his life mattered—it came to have incredible purpose—through the ministry God ordained for Ehren. The "ministry" took place in our home with caregivers who were so in love with little Ehren that their experience nursing him changed their lives in various ways. One nurse even wrote a song for Ehren. And the "ministry" took place every day that volunteers helped with Ehren's patterning therapy in the back room of the book store. Volunteers tried to help him, yet working with Ehren helped them learn and understand more about themselves.

The second part of the promise was fulfilled when Ehren died and went Home to be with his Heavenly Father. I have full faith that my son is now restored.

When Jesus called Ehren home

The night before he died, I said to Ehren, "You're going to be with God one day, and you will be so happy. You will be able to ride your little bike again and run and play with joy, just like you used to play. You'll see! You're going to feel good again when you are in Heaven."

It was Sunday morning. Hank and I were in bed. I could always hear Ehren's little handicapped cries when he woke up in his bedroom above us. I realized I had woken up to silence.

"God, I can't take one step further. Not one step. If Ehren is gone, I know he will be in Heaven with you," I prayed, weakened to the point of emotional and physical exhaustion after these eight trying years.

As I opened my eyes, a wispy white cloud came across the room, and I knew Ehren had died. Of all the visions I've had, this one brought me the most peace and closure.

I went upstairs. My expectation was confirmed. My son was finally in Heaven, lifted from his Earthly pain and suffering. I knew Ehren was whole again.

Hank ran up the steps and into Ehren's room. He turned Ehren onto his back, and we saw an ethereal smile on his face.

Hank and I didn't have to say a word. We both knew that precious, perfect smile was our sign from God that our son was Home, joyous and in perfect peace. And I know that my son has a place in Heaven because God gave His only Son, Jesus Christ, to die for our sins. In this moment of my life, everything came full circle for me. My spiritual journey had evolved to a place of personal peace in Jesus and through Jesus.

As Hank and I looked at our son, I said in a comforting, almost upbeat tone, "Ehren, this is what Mommy was talking about last night. Now you can walk and run and play again. We love you so much, and we always will love you."

Hank and I watched as Ehren's ethereal smile became a huge, radiant smile.

But it didn't end there.

We had to call the doctor, who came to our home that morning for the last time. When he saw Ehren, the doctor saw a Heavenly smile. It moved him to tears. I'll always remember seeing the doctor walking down the staircase after having seen Ehren. He was crying without shame, his face wet as he sobbed uncontrollably.

Chapter 10
8 Ways to Find Comfort After Tragedy

The eight years caring for Ehren and waiting for him to be restored were intense and inspiring, but filled with fatigue and pain. In the end, I felt like I had survived a war. I experienced flashbacks for several years after all the trauma.

After the tragedy, I needed to reconcile my feelings, learn from the sadness, and understand its impact on my spirit. I needed to release the burden and concentrate on the blessings.

There are ways to find comfort, as I've discovered over the past four decades. I think you will find these eight suggestions helpful. These have worked for me:

1. Give yourself time to heal.

Remember, I tried to write this book for decades, yet I could not. Ultimately, I met Beth, a Christian and professional writer, and she carried the burden for a few months until she wrote this book, this blessing. Beth understood that this book was one more way to heal a mother's deep pain. She prayerfully approached this, not as an assignment, but as a calling. At every turn, Beth took my feelings into account, not wanting to upset me as I re-lived all aspects of the tragedy. She understood that time heals, but a parent's grief over the loss of a child is always as painful as a fresh wound.

As you move forward, remember you need and deserve time to heal. Don't set unrealistic expectations or give yourself a timeline. Trust God's timeline for everything in life.

2. Live in the "here and now."

I wrote, "Live in the here and now" about 30 years ago. Do I "live in the here and now" every day? No. But, when I live mindfully and am present in the moment, I am most content and happy.

You can learn about *mindfulness* from many reputable sources. Simply put, practice living in the moment, not worrying about next week, next month, or next year.

3. Allow yourself to lean on others.

It's OK to ask for help, and it's smart to accept help. We hired caregivers to help meet Ehren's around-the-clock medical needs in our home, and they made it possible for us to avoid putting him in an institution. Leaning on others enabled us to have precious time with Ehren on Earth. And, as for accepting help—Where would I have been without Shirley praying me through each day? Father Paul?

So many people volunteered their time and hearts, rallying around our family. I believe they were, in turn, blessed. They found gratification through giving. Relationships such as this become mutually beneficial and uplifting.

As Second Corinthians 9:6-8 says, "Remember this: Whoever sows sparingly will also reap sparingly, and whoever sows generously will also reap generously. Each of you should **give** what you have decided in your heart to **give**, not reluctantly or under compulsion, for God loves a cheerful giver." If you are open to letting others into your life and sharing your burdens, I believe you, too, will be blessed with many cheerful givers.

4. Find joy in the simple things; they become huge things in your life.

Here's an example. After the first eight years, I had recovered enough to walk out into my back yard and pick the most wonderful French prune plums. French prune plums are small, dark skinned, oval shaped plums with a light center. Because they are small, it takes a whole lot of work to get the seeds out, cook them up, and finally get them into old-fashioned Ball canning jars. But when I had accomplished all that, it was a real joy to share the jam with special friends.

The next time you lose the ability to find joy in the simple things, remember those wonderful little plums and how I literally bottled my joy to share with others.

5. Serve others.

I volunteered at Casa Serena for five years. After Ehren's death, I served children in Uganda. I found that it helped immensely to get outside of myself and focus on those less fortunate.

When Ehren died, my pastor called me into his office. He mentioned that something had come across his desk, and he believed it was for me. The Big Shootout is an organization that had been going to East Africa since the 1960s to immunize children up to five years of age.

Since I had gone back to college to get my RN degree before Ehren was born, I was eligible to go. Father Paul said he believed Ehren would love for me to go and help these poor children. I went to the heart of Uganda for a life-changing adventure (but that is another story).

6. Pray.

I was afraid some people wouldn't read this section if "prayer" was first on the list. My prayer warriors were and continue to be an integral part of my life. Pray unceasingly, as the Bible says. Therein, you will find comfort and peace.

7. Get counseling.

Healthcare professionals counsel people through many traumas. During and after the trauma, you can benefit from their expert training. It's a good idea to begin with your primary care physician, who can recommend the right practitioner. You may be referred to a psychologist, psychiatrist, or another counseling resource in your area.

There should be no stigma attached to mental health concerns. Getting help for your mental health should be as natural and easy as getting help for a broken arm or indigestion.

8. Read the Bible.

God's Holy Word is a light for us all. The next chapter is devoted to showing you how.

Chapter 11
WHERE TO FIND YOUR BLESSING

One day, a voice came into my heart saying, "Open your Bible." I listened.

I opened my Bible to Luke and was guided to Zacharias' Song. (Luke 1:67-80)

Each time I searched the scriptures, Ehren was on my mind. Of course, he still is foremost in my mind when I read the Bible or talk with God. That's the nature of enduring tragedy. Parents never forget and probably never really let go.

Now, I understand that Zacharias' Song or Prophecy is the story of John's promised birth. Zacharias and his wife, Mary, who believed she was barren, were promised a son, whom they should name John.

Beginning in the first chapter of Luke, the Virgin Mary's miraculous calling to be the mother of Jesus is also recounted. We read that Mary, the Mother of Jesus, came to live with Zacharias and Mary for "about three months, and returned to her own house." (Luke 1:56)

Soon, John was born. And, in contrast to what others around her said, his mother Mary said, "he shall be called John." (Luke 1:60)

So, although I understand the Biblical story, when I opened my Bible in the 1970s and it fell open to Luke 1:67-80, I applied the words to Ehren. Yes, I know this text was not written all those thousands of years ago just for Ehren. But I do know that the Bible speaks to all humankind as well today as it did the moment it was written, thus its role as our *Living* Bible. And I found special comfort in the verses I read that day:

> [67] And his father Zacharias was filled with the Holy Ghost, and prophesied, saying,
>
> [68] Blessed be the Lord God of Israel; for he hath visited and redeemed his people,
>
> [69] And hath raised up an horn of salvation for us in the house of his servant David;
>
> [70] As he spake by the mouth of his holy prophets, which have been since the world began:

⁷¹ That we should be saved from our enemies, and from the hand of all that hate us;

⁷² To perform the mercy promised to our fathers, and to remember his holy covenant;

⁷³ The oath which he swore to our father Abraham,

⁷⁴ That he would grant unto us, that we being delivered out of the hand of our enemies might serve him without fear,

⁷⁵ In holiness and righteousness before him, all the days of our life.

⁷⁶ And thou, child, shalt be called the prophet of the Highest: for thou shalt go before the face of the Lord to prepare his ways; !!!!

⁷⁷ To give knowledge of salvation unto his people by the remission of their sins,

> **⁷⁸** Through the tender mercy of our God; whereby the dayspring from on high hath visited us,
>
> **⁷⁹** To give light to them that sit in darkness and in the shadow of death, to guide our feet into the way of peace.
>
> **⁸⁰** And the child grew, and waxed strong in spirit, and was in the deserts till the day of his shewing unto Israel.
>
> -King James Version

That day, I felt Ehren was in the desert because of his disabilities, and when he was completely restored, he would be telling people about the Lord.

I believe the same thing today, but in a different context. Now I know that people came to know the Lord Jesus as their Savior because of Ehren's disabilities through his patterning therapy, before he was completely restored in Heaven.

I was drawn to the word "dayspring," a lovely word, but a source of debate among theologians. Some believe the "dayspring from on high" in <u>verse 78</u> is Jesus Christ. Others, such as <u>Jeremy Myers</u>, believe dayspring is "the branch of light which comes before the sun. It is the few minutes of light right before the first rays of sun appear on the horizon. In this context, it appears that Zacharias believes his son John is this light, the forerunner to the actual Light of the world."

Understanding that people contemplate and even debate Biblical verses in such a way helped me appreciate their value in my everyday life. Perhaps it's OK for me to find meaning—and comfort—when I open the Bible to a collection of verses to which God led me. As I read the Bible, some passages would jump out at me and have such meaning for that particular day. I appreciate receiving those blessings from God through His Word.

Luke verses 78, 79, and 80 brought me comfort. There is joy in the thought that *through the tender mercy of our God*, Ehren, who was sitting *in darkness and in the shadow of death* for eight years, was visited by the dayspring of light from on high and guided on his feet (restored and able to move his legs and arms again!) to perfect peace. Through God, I believe my child grew *and became strong in spirit and was taken from the desert* to be with the God of Israel . . . our God.

"There are times," I wrote, that I would "be absolutely blown away by what the Bible would say."

I encourage everyone to read the Bible, study, and pray about what you've read. Pray for understanding, guidance, and an increasingly deeper faith in God. I also encourage everyone to join with other believers whenever possible; I have found great value in prayer groups.

In order to really hear what God is telling us, we must invite Him to do so. This isn't as complicated as many people would like to believe. In fact, there is nothing complicated about God or His Word.

All you have to do is simply ask.

To ask Jesus into your life as your personal Savior, the Bible says in Romans 10:9 10:

> 9 If you declare with your mouth, "Jesus is Lord," and believe in your heart that God raised him from the dead, you will be saved.
>
> 10 For it is with your heart that you believe and are justified, and it is with your mouth that you profess your faith and are saved.

Here are some additions I would like to add just before publicatuion:

PREPARE

Prepare hearts minds and souls for what is coming.

I saw a great wheel. It had spokes of old wood. It was moving. It was manned by unknowns to me. It definitely causing mayhem..

The key of David was given to me as something very important. That is for someone else to interpret as a possible prophecy for end times.

THE ROOM

For some reason, the doctors had requested Ehren to be moved from the Pediatric section to downstairs that adjoined a hallway and the room where people could go and pray and rest and wait for a word for their loved ones.

From my home I drove to the hospital my heart and my stomach just not knowing what was happening and remembering the words that God had told me, I think because of that I knew in my heart that whatever happened everything was going to be OK. I guess you would call it a blind faith but after hearing an audible word from God there's just nothing else in the whole world that you can do but believe, so I arrived and my friend Jay was to meet me and sit with me in that room just waiting to hear what the doctors were saying about his recovery. I couldn't understand, they still wouldn't let me go in that room and I'm still sitting there thinking about all of this and all of a sudden I hear Unknown caller No coming through all the four walls heavenly music. I thought who is turning music on in this room. it wasn't loud but I could hear it and then when Jay walked in and I said listen can't you hear that music and she just went to all four walls and she couldn't hear anything but I kept insisting I heard … while this was going on a pastor from the Lutheran Church came in to say prayers over Ehren all of a sudden Ehren's cry were like a real baby's cry not the brain injured cry that we had been hearing for days. the pastor knocked on the door and we opened it up and he was sobbing just crying his heart out. I told him about the music and Jay mentioned she had heard something similar about heavenly music coming to people.

REVELATION TO TITLE OF MY BOOK

I think for years ever since God gave me the message that the title of my book would be my burden my blessing, I had sort of tucked away in my mind that he did mean Ehren was my burden but I couldn't completely go along with that in my head as I felt on one hand, so blessed. It was such a dichotomy. here my child was severely injured but I still loved him to pieces. I can't totally explain my feelings as here was my child totally incapacitated but at the same time I'm feeling blessed and the reason for that is because I heard the audible word of God!! How can you not feel that you are so blessed when something like that occurs. I finally came to the realization that my burden, my burden was the fact that I wanted to go out and tell the world everything that had occurred concerning the audible voice, the vision. I think God waited to have me finish this book for his perfect timing. Now I understand going to person to person hoping somebody would listen to my story and they write my book. One girl tried to write my story but she put too much of herself into it and it just wasn't right. Now so many years has gone by and the world in 2024 is completely falling apart. not just the United States but worldwide, it's like Sodom and Gomorra. I have no idea what God has in store for me but all I can do is lift up to him what is in my heart and definitely not making money but sharing my miracle stories is the ultimate for me. AMEN

MY LAST ENTRIES TO MY BURDEN MY BLESSING

Back in the 80s when I was in prayer groups when I was marking up my Bible, I had many entries or I should say underlining in my Bible of passages that I felt were very prophetic for Ehren And myself. I'm going to list them because they all spoke to me but there may be somebody out there that they also speak to. for some reason God gave me prophetic messages for Jewish people. Ones that don't believe in Jesus as their savior. I have many Jewish friends and we never talk Religion. I can talk about it in my book thank God. I will list here as I went through my Bible and wrote them down to type in here:

Psalm 3 Verse 4 January 1983

Psalm four verse 4 January 1983

Jeremiah 29 verse 11 through 13 1980

Luke 1 zacharias prophecy 67 through 80. This was for Ehren

John 10. verse 16. Message to Jewish people.

Revelations 3 Versus seven through 13 January 18 1980. This was given to me especially what the Jewish people.

Revelations 12 verses 1-18 Verse 17 is very pertinent to me in recent history as the devil reared his head and created a horrible situation with my son and daughter. Personally I believe the Bible is full of wisdom and truth for everyday living and not only just historical.

CATHOLIC PRIEST PROPHECY FOR EHREN

"EHREN WILL USHER IN THE SECOND COMING OF JESUS CHRIST"

Somewhere between the years 1978 through 1984 that was the prophecy that came to my Bible group teacher. I went to the Holy Land with my Catholic priest Bible group teacher. no one knew I was not Catholic but father Jim knew my heart. I joined in on a three or five day novena to Saint Theresa of lisieux. We're told we would smell or see or be given a rose during those days. that actually happened when we first arrived in Rome the most outstanding rose that happened was when a group of us got lost in Rome and could not find our way back to our hotel. we saw a priest coming out of a small church we hailed him down and told him we were lost and could he direct us to our hotel. The priest said of course but first come into my church. that church was dedicated to Saint Theresa of lisieux. Even her body was there under a glass case uncorrupted.

This is the end of my book to you. God Bless

Mollie Edwards

MY BURDEN MY BLESSING

Uganda mission. Paid by my Church after Ehren passed.

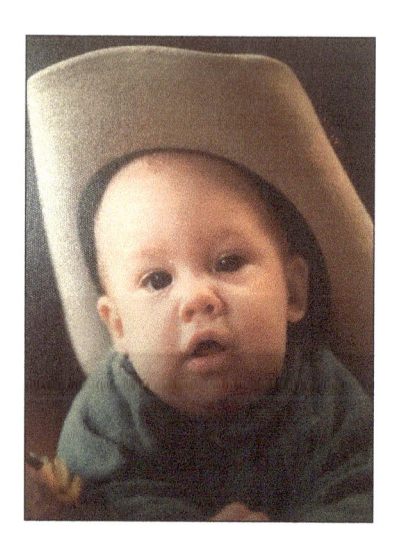

Ehren as a baby

Where to Find Your Blessing

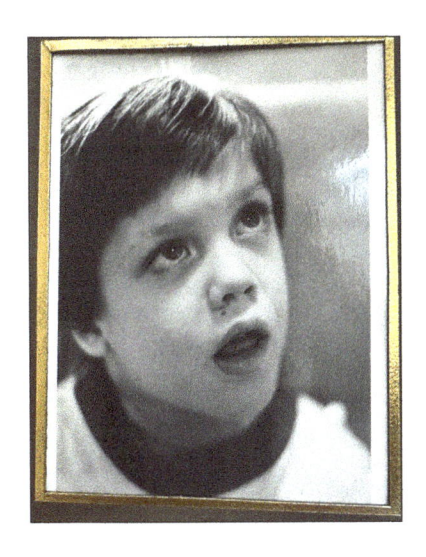

Ehren after accident

Mollie and Hank parents of Ehren

MY BURDEN MY BLESSING

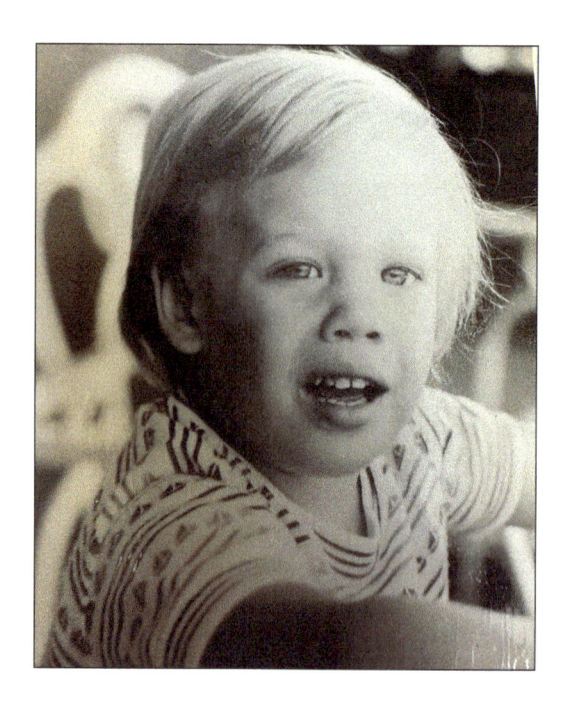

A month before accident

A REMEMBRANCE

Within a month or two after Ehren's accident the movie Jesus Of Nazareth came out on television. I called my Mom because I felt a message from God telling me I would learn more about my Vision from the movie.

When in the movie Lazarus stepped out of tomb with cloth flying around I turned towards my Mom who had come to my home to watch movie with me and I said "OK tell me about that cloth around Lazarus", My Mom said a winding cloth when someone died back then. If a new born it was called a swaddling cloth. At death the same cloth head to toe.

I went back in my mind to my vision and I immediately remembered seeing something I could not understand at the time. I saw winds from head to toe around bundle that was offered down to me.

Everything God said in that unheard of voice. "Ehren will come back to you, Ehren will be restored ", was exactly true. Ehren Died, he was caught up in

Heaven, he was given back to earth for his mission and was restored back to God.

A huge thanks to Beth Lombardi who many years ago heard my story in a writers group. She felt God tugging at her heart to help me edit and finish my book that had been written many years prior. She completed that mission and that work sat for many more years until I felt the nudging of God, it was time to publish. 2024 actually marks the fourth decade since the Death of Ehren. My only prayer is that my vision and heavenly words from God will Bless whoever reads this tiny book.

May the God of hope fill you with all joy and peace as you trust in him, so that you may overflow with hope by the power of the Holy Spirit. <u>Romans 15:13</u> | <u>NIV</u>

Milton Keynes UK
Ingram Content Group UK Ltd.
UKHW051653081024
449373UK00018B/232